Crisis Hunter: The last flight of Joseph P. Kennedy Jr

PAUL ELGOOD

Columbia Point
Brighton, UK

FOR WAYNE

Also by Paul Elgood

Kennedy at Birch Grove

CONTENTS

CHRONOLGY

25 July 1915 – Joe Kennedy Jr born, Brookline, Massachusetts

1938 – Joe Jr first arrived in London, as son of Ambassador Joseph P. Kennedy

1940 – Joe Jr's departure for the United States, Law School

24 June 1941 – Joe Jr enlisted in the US Navy Reserve, Boston, Mass

15 July 1941- Joe Jr reported for basic training as a US Navy Pilot

6 June 1944 – Having returned to England, Joe Jr provided air support during the D-Day landings

13 June 1944 – The first German V-1 rocket hits London

25 July 1944 – Joe Jr volunteered for secret operation

30 July 1944 – Joe Jr travelled to Fersfield to begin training

12 August 1944 – The fatal mission, ending above Suffolk, England

1 January 1945 - JFK published *"As We Remember Joe"*

5 November 1946 – JFK elected to Congress for the first time

Source: JFK Library

Joe Kennedy Jr.
Credit: JFK Library/copy from the author's collection

"It has been said that time heals all wounds. I don't agree. The wounds remain. Time covers them and the pain lessens, but it is never gone."

Mrs Rose Kennedy

"A wound that does not heal."

Senator Teddy Kennedy

"For the last ten days I have been stuck out in the country, far beyond striking distance of any town. Every day, I think will be my last here, and still we go on. I am really fed up, but the work is quite interesting. The nature of it is secret, and you know how secret things are in the Navy."

Joseph Kennedy Jr, in his final letter to his brother JFK, 10th August 1944

"One by one the factors which might have caused the explosion were studied by investigators, but no final conclusion as to the cause was reached."

US Navy Department statement, 24th October 1945

PREFACE

High expectations were placed on the first born son of Joseph and Rose Kennedy.

In the wake of his support for the pre-war policy of appeasement, Ambassador Joseph P. Kennedy knew he would never be President. He seamlessly transferred his ambition to his children, anointing the oldest, Joe Jr, as his proxy for the White House. Joe Jr was living the Ivy League life of the east coast social elite until the call to England interrupted his idyllic lifestyle as President Roosevelt appointed the elder Kennedy to be his ambassador to England. Joseph Kennedy Sr placed huge pressure on Joe Jr, instilling his Irish American insecurities on his son to always compete and win. In peace and war, Joe Jr's pursuit of excellence propelled him forward. War hero was the next expectation placed on him.

After two tours of duty in war-weary England, Joe Jr had flown enough combat missions to make him eligible to return home, his war over. Instead, Joe volunteered to stay in England, taking on even greater risks piloting dangerous missions to target Hitler's devastating V-bombing campaign. By August 1944, he stepped forward to co-pilot the launch of a top secret perhaps near suicidal drone bombing mission. Departing from RAF Fersfield in Suffolk, the flight went badly wrong and the plane exploded shortly after take-off. The crew's bodies were never found.

Eyewitnesses described two explosions and a huge ball of fire with debris scattered for at least a mile. However, mystery surrounded the mission Joe Jr gave his life for and it took decades for details to be declassified. Even the official letters to his powerful father gave little detail away. Writing years later, his brother Senator Ted Kennedy recalled:

> "After completing his required twenty-five combat missions and earning his right to return home, Joe had volunteered for a mission so dangerous that some of his ground crew pleaded with him not to go. Along with a co-pilot, he was to take off in an experimental drone loaded with high explosives and pilot it on a trajectory toward a target...Whatever the cause, the drone had exploded into a fireball just minutes before the two pilots were due to bail out."[1]

The word hero is often overused, but in Joe Jr's case it is entirely justified. The Commander of the United States Navy wrote to Joseph Kennedy Sr to console the distraught parents, telling them "...to be very proud of your son for his courage, his devotion to duty, and the magnificent example he has set for the rest of us". The Navy Cross, Distinguished Flying Cross and the Air Medal were awarded for "extraordinary heroism", but were in reality little consolation to the father for losing his first son.

Joe Jr's likely place in Congress and the Senate were taken by his younger brother, John F. Kennedy, who went onto fulfil their father's dream in 1960 to see a Kennedy enter the White House. A thousand days later he too was killed in the line of duty, and by 1968 Bobby, the third brother had fallen. The events of the war years would cast a long shadow over the family for decades to come. Veteran White House correspondent Helen Thomas wrote:

"John Kennedy understood his time was short, that he had a rendezvous with death. The deaths of a sister and brother during World War Two, as well as the horrors of war he experienced in the South Pacific, may have given him a sense of melancholy and foreboding."[2]

As a Senator, John himself wrote "I'm only trying to fill his shoes...If anything happened to me tomorrow, Bobby would run for my seat in the Senate. And if Bobby died, our younger brother Teddy would take over." This was the prolongation of what would become known as the "Kennedy Imprisonment".

The Kennedy Family in London in 1938, Joe Jr is fourth from the right. Credit: JFK Library/copy from the author's collection.

It is now seventy years since the events of August 1944 took place. Sightings of the wreckage of the plane were last recorded in the late seventies. Yet during the intervening years the remains of the drone aircraft have been relatively undisturbed as they lay scattered across remote woodland in the Suffolk countryside, remaining a well-kept local secret.

"It is hard to believe it all happened seventy years ago now", said one crew member stationed at the same airbase as Joe Jr. A Democratic Convention tribute to the late Senator Ted Kennedy recalled the tragedy as "a wound that does not heal". Today, except to those in his family and the few surviving veterans, the sacrifice of what took place in August 1944 is near forgotten.

CHAPTER 1

Had it not been for the second world war, Joe Kennedy Jr might have been President. As the oldest of Joseph Kennedy Sr and Rose Kennedy's children, he was the sibling first in line to fulfil the presidential ambitions of their father. Joe Jr's early life was spent as part of a large and wealthy Irish American family in Brookline, Boston. Schooled at the elite Dexter, Brookline and Choate schools, he graduated from Harvard in 1938. Joe Jr stood out amongst his contemporaries, even taking his first political steps in politics as a delegate at the 1940 Democratic Convention.[3]

The Kennedy children were notoriously competitive, derived in part by the racism Irish Americans faced at the time. Joe Sr instilled in his children the desire to win. The family narrative follows this from touch football on the front lawn of their Hyannis Port home to their heated debates at family meal times, Kennedy's children were taught to compete, stand their ground and always be the best. The sibling rivalry between Joe Jr and his brother John was most acute. Joe Jr was the older brother to but lacked the intellect and early promise of his younger sibling in the classroom. John out performed his older brother at school and college; John top of his class and Joe Jr initially struggling and two hundredth in his. The pressure just kept building on Joe Jr.

Joseph P. Kennedy Sr came from Boston Irish stock. Ambitious, brash and confrontational, he was not one to take hostages. Writer Thurston Clarke speculates that the Kennedys were probably the richest Irish

American family in the country, and that Joe Sr raised his family in the ways of old-Boston Brahmins, the traditional east coast upper class white elite.[4] Before Joe Sr, the Kennedys were already well established in Boston politics, however Joe Sr wanted wealth and power on a national even international scale and well beyond the state of Massachusetts. As Joe Sr took his opportunities to make money - he was said to have profited from the Wall Street Crash and Prohibition, not to mention the growing film industry of the 1920's. He also took advantage politically by supporting President Roosevelt as he won the Democratic nomination for President, and subsequently the White House, as he took office in 1933. Kennedy was rewarded with public office, but there were tensions between the two men, Kennedy being an obvious threat to the President.

The pinnacle of Kennedy Sr's political career came as Ambassador to London, the Court of St James, putting him at the forefront of the escalating tensions of Europe in the late 1930's. Roosevelt's man in London increasingly took an isolationist stance to the rise of Hitler and the fascists. What seems beyond question is Joe Sr's devotion to his children. Throughout their lives the Kennedy children always paid due respect to their father, even when themselves in high office. His fear over the escalation of war during the late 1930's perhaps can be explained by Joe Sr knowing that America would inevitably be sucked into any conflict which emerged, and with that his family. These fears turned into reality, even beyond his own apprehensions.

Mrs Rose Kennedy shared her husband's devotion to their children. For Rose it was expressed through her Catholic faith; for Joe Sr through power and money. Whilst Joe was building his network of power, wealth and influence, Rose very much stayed behind bringing up the stream of Kennedy children. Rose spoke much about her family and especially her children, however seemed oblivious to much of what Joe Sr was up to. In her oral history to the JFK Library, for her autobiography, she seemed to deny any philandering on her husband's part. She even laughed at rumours circulating from the time that Joe Sr's affair with film actress Gloria Swanson resulted in an illegitimate child.[5]

Joe Jr, Joe Sr and JFK en route to London in 1938.
Credit: JFK Library/copy from the author's collection.

England was to play a decisive role in Joe Jr's life and indeed that of his family. In 1938 the ambitious patriarch uprooted his family to take up his post as ambassador, putting the Kennedys in frontline London during the period immediately before the outbreak of war and the tense early months of the conflict. But, as was often the case with the Kennedys, even as war approached, the family dazzled English society and were entertained by Royalty, politicians and coveted by the press. The older siblings spent much of their time on England's social circuit, taking London society by storm. As David Blunkett, writing in 2013, put it:

> "In many respects this was a free and easy time for those born into money, and in this case it was the coming together of the British aristocracy and the US equivalent, in what had become known as the Kennedy clan."[6]

However, they also found time to follow the more serious events of the day, with the brothers watching most of the historic developments on the eve of war unfold from the gallery of the House of Commons. Joe Jr acted as political aide to his father, as ambassador, giving him a unique insight into the escalating tensions, and he had studied for a year under socialist Harold Laski at the London School of Economics.[7] Rose Kennedy recalled that during this time Joe Jr even went to Russia on a field trip and came back "full of socialist ideas".[8] Had these youthful opinions developed further for Joe Jr, perhaps America might have been looking at its first President with socialist leanings. A memorable student, Laski himself recalled Joe Jr well, he remarked;

> "Three things, above all, stand out in my recollection of young Joe in that year. Above all, his astonishing vitality. He was interested in everything... second, there was his astonishing capacity for enthusiasm. What he liked, he liked with all his heart. The third thing was his profound interest in politics. He had set his heart on a political career; he has often sat in my study and submitted with that smile that was pure magic to relentless teasing

about his determination to be nothing less than President of the United States."

In *"As We Remember Joe"* John F. Kennedy recalled that Joe Jr had spent 1939 travelling through Europe. Joe Jr, his brother wrote, was in Czechoslovakia at the time of the Munich pact, and was in Madrid when the city fell to Franco. Joe Jr's first experience of war did indeed come in Spain during its civil war. Joe Sr used his sons as "political scouts" to report on the ground about developments in mainland Europe, however Joe Sr had not wanted his sons so close to the frontline in Spain. Joe Sr had told the *'New York Times"* that his eldest son was just "having a look around". Joe Jr arrived in a deserted Valencia, devastated by bombing. It was here that he experienced his first air-raid, watching Franco's bombers drop their loads on the harbour front. Joe Jr had headed for the action, rather than to safety, a habit he would develop. Reneham wrote that:

> "The Ambassador should not have been surprised by Joe Jr's attraction to the fatal grounds of war torn Spain. The same young man who so often bloodied himself on the football and rugby field...had long seemed compulsively drawn to danger." [9]

Joe Jr wrote in *'The Atlantic"* on the 15th February 1939, from Valencia that the port was one of the most devastated things he'd ever seen. Joe Jr reported that "every house within a radius of half a mile is a litter of wreckage". Describing the air-raid, he wrote;

> "The noise was terrific. It made our ears ache. The building vibrated like drums...The din lasted for about five minutes; then complete silence. The thing that got me was the feeling

of absolute helplessness There's not a thing you can do about it all."

He made it through to Barcelona and stayed for a lengthy period in Madrid, where he was the only American known to be in the city at that point of the conflict. One morning he awoke to find Franco's soldiers posted on every street corner. Madrid had capitulated, with Joe Jr at its very heart, whilst his sibling John only made it as far as the French border before being turned back.[10] A *"New York Times"* headline from 17th February 1939 screamed "son of Kennedy visits besieged Madrid; "Just Looking Around" says Ambassador". Already Joe Jr was in the public eye, and his exploits reported back to the American public by a canny Joe Sr. The report stated that Joe Jr had arrived in Madrid the day before, just as the shelling had stopped. Arrangements were made to put him up at the empty United States Embassy building "where he could learn for himself what it was like to live in a besieged city on a diet of sardines and rice". Joe Jr, the report follows, had travelled from Valencia that afternoon on a special bus chartered by the government. Joe Jr had written his Harvard thesis on the Spanish Non-Intervention Committee and wanted to take a look at the country, the article stated. All Joe Sr received was a cable from Joe Jr. "Sorry I missed you Stop Arrived safely in Valencia Stop Going Madrid tonight Regards Joe."[11]

"The New York Times" reported that Joe Sr had said that the younger Joe's adventures "were nothing new". Risk-taking started to become a habit for Joe Jr, with the London newspapers from the time labelling him a "crisis hunter". In the weeks before war he witnessed Berlin, Rome and Paris at first hand; noting that there was little concern over war in Germany, but

for the French unease was clearly evident on the streets.[12] But then as Joe Sr firmly put it, "...he is going back to Cambridge to the Harvard Law School in the Fall." At which point his father put to an end Joe Jr's pre-war European adventures. *"The New York Herald-Tribune"* had also picked the story up from the Associated Press, adding Joe Sr as saying: "his mother will die when she hears he is in Madrid", calling him a "student of crisis".[13]

The Ambassador's time in London would cast a long shadow over the reputation of the Kennedy family. By instinct Joe Sr was an isolationist, bitterly opposed to the prospect of a conflict and the growing likelihood of a long and bloody war led the elder Kennedy to argue for a course of appeasement against Hitler, about whom he had expressed some early admiration for. As for many Americans, the prospect of conflict seemed distant and little to do with them, literally an ocean away between the old and new worlds. Rapidly events began to take their dramatic course as public opinion in England turned against the failed appeasement of the Nazis and with it the gradual realisation by President Roosevelt that America would only be able to stay out of war for so long. Once Roosevelt had the 1940 election behind him, and as Hitler marched through Europe, war in Europe became increasingly unavoidable for the Americans. The world would need to act.

Whilst Joe Sr became increasingly out of step with opinion in Britain, perhaps his motivation could partly be explained due to his overriding concern for the safety of his sons. His was the generation who lived in the wake of the Great War and he must have known that any war would drag two of his boys into the frontline of the conflict. He was cautious for their welfare, and seemed desperate to protect them. In the same way during the early stages of the conflict he had sent his family for periods to Scotland and Ascot, near Windsor, even when the British Royals stayed at Buckingham Palace to remain in London during the blitz.

On the eve of war: Joe Jr, Kathleen and JFK heading to the House of Commons to hear the war declaration debate on 3rd September 1939.
Credit: JFK Library/copy from the author's collection

The Kennedys stayed in England for the outbreak of hostilities. Like other families living in London at the time, they made preparations for the imminent conflict. On the day war was declared they sheltered in the Embassy basement, waiting for the first air-raid, which famously failed to come. At that stage of the war, Americans in London were bystanders to the escalating conflict, Joe Kennedy Sr's support for appeasement and early sympathy for Hitler, put him out of step with the country's inevitable march to war. By the time Churchill as Prime Minister rallied the country to counter the threat from Nazi Germany, the language of appeasement sounded near treasonous and outdated. War was consuming Europe, and the British had no choice but to defend their freedom. By picking no side, Joe Sr looks to history that he had picked the wrong side.

By late 1940, with the growing split between the Ambassador and President Roosevelt, the Kennedys left London. For Joe Jr it was for a year at law school, but he would return to fight in the conflict which his father had sought so hard to avoid. Rose Kennedy wrote to a friend, apprehensive of her sons impending military service: "...these are really tragic days but we are very thankful that we have Joe and Jack still in this country."[14] Soon her boys would be gone to war.

CHAPTER 2

It took until late 1943 for Joe Jr to arrive back in England, and by then he had a point to prove. Europe was now four years into war, with the conflict starting to turn in favour of the Allies. Joe Jr was determined to head into action quickly, as until that point his pilot's training had kept him out of harm's way on exercises in north America. It was a different story for his brother, John F. Kennedy, or Jack, who literally found himself running into the Japanese whist stationed in the Pacific. John's heroism increased Joe Jr's determination to equal his sibling's combat record, and that meant Joe taking risks to keep pace.

Ensign Joseph P. Kennedy Jr, 1942.

Credit: JFK Library.

John Kennedy had captained a small Navy PT109 cruiser vessel, which saw direct action in the Soloman Islands. His craft was rammed by a Japanese destroyer, sinking his vessel and leaving the crew adrift for a week. In the end John summoned help by sending a message written on a coconut shell, saving the lives of his injured crew. Back home Joe Sr took every opportunity to promote his second son's courage under fire; perhaps to atone for his own position on appeasement at the outbreak of war. Joe Sr knew that the word "appeaser" would be used against his family, and that this would be political suicide for the next generation of his family trying to assume elected office. Joe Sr had begun to create a myth around his boys which he intended to fully exploit during their subsequent political campaigns.

Having completed his training, Joe Jr returned to England, landing at St Eval in Cornwall. His physical examination papers called him "athletic, erect, heavy frames".[15] He flew himself across the Atlantic in a convoy in which one plane developed engine trouble and had only just reached its destination. The remote west country was a backwater compared to the bright lights of pre-war London he saw when he last arrived in England, during what by then must have seemed a long gone era. Whilst only a few years apart, the difference between peacetime and wartime England could not have been more extreme. He last arrived in London at the height of the thirties, during the period directly ahead of the outbreak of war. Perhaps then, his generation had little concept of the enormity of what would face them a few years hence, making his time in pre-war London considerably different to the England he returned to in 1943. Now, he was met with a country defending itself against the Nazi threat, putting up with rationing shortages and living every day with the fear and dread that war held. Moreover, the geographical differences of the two locations made them feel half a century apart; the rural south west seeming far from the dangers of the frontline.

This was another backwater posting for a young pilot with a lot to prove and an urgency to prove it.

With his arrival training behind him, Joe Jr moved to Dunkeswell airfield in Devon, where he fell under the direction of the RAF's Coastal Command, overseeing the Bay of Biscay and the south eastern Atlantic. Joe would undertake U-boat patrols, clocking up his flying hours with relative ease; but due to the vast area of ocean it covered the posting offered him minimal contact with the enemy. Whilst a step closer to the action, these repetitive and remote missions kept him away from danger, increasing his frustration at not having the opportunity to match his brother's heroism. Joe Jr yearned to be closer to the action and to make a name for himself as a heroic war pilot. With John's war record in the bag, the pressure increased on Joe Jr with every letter home.

RAF Dunkeswell today (public domain photograph).

On one occasion, Joe Jr picked up a Messerschmitt on his tail, which tagged his American PB4Y bomber aircraft for a time, causing the aircraft to open fire in defence. After some aerobatics from the German plane, the attacker was off. Joe Jr continued the mission undeterred but with his bomb load intact – his orders stated that he should have ditched it at the first sign of danger. As the squadron clocked up their missions, and even as casualties occurred, Joe Jr still remained one step away from the direct combat that he craved.

During those months in the south west, Joe Jr spent time with his sister Kathleen, known as Kick. They would exchange visits, with Joe Jr heading to London at every possible opportunity. The two Kennedy siblings spent as much time together as possible and that their respective war duties would allow. Kathleen Kennedy worked for the Red Cross in London and married the Duke of Devonshire's son, Billy Hartington, Joe Jr being the only Kennedy family member attending. Even during wartime the younger Kennedys remained very much at the heart of the British establishment, picking up with the same social group as they were with during their father's time as Ambassador. This ready-made social set would follow them all the way to the White House.

Joe Jr though settled into his arduous flying posting during the long winter of 1943 and 1944. His talent was quickly recognised by his commanding officers, one of whom, J. R. Reedy wrote on 22nd December 1943 of "the splendid performance of duty" of the unit that Joe Jr was part of. Reedy acknowledged their devotion to duty and maintenance of high standards under "trying circumstances and rigorous conditions". The unit had demonstrated the "courage", Joe Jr had been so keen to extoll.[16]

In a report later used in *"As We Remember Joe"* on 29th December 1943, radio correspondent Arthur Mann reported from the base. From his experiences there, he stated;

> "The men who fly these planes are part of the secret, silent, battle of the Atlantic against

German U-Boats; a battle which goes on twenty-four hours a day for 365 days in the year."

He described their living quarters as Nissen huts and muddy fields, supported by a mess and cafeteria run by the W.A.A.F. These "girls" also joined the men in dances, films, walks and entertainment shows, such was the boredom of the crews at the isolated base, he stated. Mann went on;

"Shortly before dinner in came the pilot of the plane in which I was to go. He was Joseph P. Kennedy Jr, son of the former American Ambassador to Great Britain. "Coming to the movie after dinner," he asked me; "It's *'Eagle Squadron'*." I very firmly declined remarking, "Joe, a man who goes to see a flying film just before starting out on a twelve-hour hop is certainly a glutton for punishment."

Joe Jr's opportunity for heroism finally came in the spring of 1944 during the preparations for D-Day. Allied commanders saw it as essential to keep the invasion fleet free from sea-born attack, countering the threat of German U-Boats or their boat patrols from the west. Joe's squadron was the only one available for deployment to fight on this front, and who knew the geography well enough to be an effective defence against such attack. On D-Day itself Joe Jr patrolled the area to the west of the invasion fleet, in the crucial western area that the U-Boats might threaten to approach from. He would have observed the fleet from a safe distance, as the largest seaborne invasion force in history and on their way to liberate the beaches of Normandy from the Nazis. By the third day, Joe Jr still had limited direct contact with the enemy, although he had provided key intelligence to keep the invasion fleet safe from U-

Boat attack from the west. This would never be enough for Joe Jr, in a time of war heroes, and he just kept flying, waiting for the right opportunity to prove himself. By the end of the month, whilst an exhausted Joe Jr and his crew had flown daily, twelve hour sorties, as Searls put it: "...the invasion fleet lost not a single ship to a U-Boat in the entire month of June."[17]

Joe Jr, could soon go home, his mission completed and having been part of the historic invasion of Europe, but unlike his brother John, it would mean that he would return home without the stories of heroism that he so craved, and which he could talk about during family lunches at Hyannis Port. Instead he volunteered to stay in England, to take on the next opportunity before him for heroism. In paying tribute to his brother, John F. Kennedy wrote:

> "His squadron, flying in the bitter winter over the Bay of Biscay, suffered heavy casualties, and by the time Joe had completed his designated number of missions in May, he had lost his former co-pilot and a number of close friends. Joe refused his proffered leave and persuaded his crew to remain on for D-day. They flew frequently during June and July, and at the end of July they were given another opportunity to go home. He felt it unfair to ask his crew to stay on longer, and they returned to the United States. He remained. For he had heard of a new and special assignment for which volunteers had been requested which would require another month of the most dangerous type of flying."18

As Joe Jr marshalled the Normandy landings from the air, another event was taking place in London which would subsequently put him in the way of danger. On

13th June 1944, and prompted by the D-Day landings itself, Adolf Hitler unleashed the first of his deadly V-bombing campaigns on London. At its peak over 9,000 V-1 bombs were fired at London, and British Intelligence knew that V-1 was only one part of a devastating Nazi programme of aerial bombings, which would terrify a near defenceless London. The Nazis were in the process of developing the V-2 guided missile, which would be operational by the end of August 1944 and the V-3 canons would follow, both of which Hitler hoped would devastate the capital and help him regain the initiative in the wake of the Allied landings, literally holding the British to ransom against the Allied advance across Europe. The size and power of the V-2 meant that the missiles touched the edge of space, before descending at 400 miles an hour at an 80 degree angle, making them near impossible to shoot down once fired. Hitler was targeting civilian causalities to reduce morale of war-weary Britain and open-up a new front for the Germans. Moreover, this new form of attack was Hitler's revenge for the Allied attacks on mainland Europe.

Instead of returning to America, his duty completed, Joe Jr stepped forward for a dangerous secret mission which he was told had the potential to turn the tide of the war. Operation Aphrodite or Anvil, as the Army and Navy secret code-names respectively called it would target the V-missile sites on the coast of Normandy, and attempt to take-out the heavily defended launch sites. What made the operation different and so secret was the use of unmanned drone aircraft, filled with high explosives, which would literally dive-bomb the sites. These would be crewed by pilots who would bailout prior to the bombing phase of the flight. The adapted bombers were stripped back to be as light as possible and to enable the loading of approximately 25,000 pounds of Torpex explosives. The wings of the planes were painted a ghostly white, to enable easier control by the accompanying aircraft, or "mother ships". The Navy's interest in the project included the possible deployment of the technique in the war in the pacific, perhaps to counter the deadly menace of Japanese kamikaze attacks.

The crew working at Dunkeswell included waist gunner Walt Pugsley, now living in Randolph, New Jersey and aged 89 years. He was based there with John Dumont, also now 89, of Peterstown; David Smith, 90, of Proctorville, Ohio and Bill Bizzell, of Cleveland, Miss. The crew still meet up to this day. Walt remembers well the task of bringing the bombers over from the US, and then reducing the weight as far as possible. He worked on Joe Jr's actual plane, but knew little of the reason for their efforts or the mission being undertaken. Even with those working within the base, the purpose for their work was not discussed. Nearly seventy years on, he still speaks of his sadness of the loss of the two pilots on the mission. He had followed a similar wartime journey to Joe Jr in the Navy, undertaking the long and laborious missions to counter the D-Day U-Boat threat, rarely seeing the enemy from the air. What he remembers is the unique feeling of the time, arriving in England in June 1944 he was stationed in England during the final phase of the war. It was an exciting time for him, or any young man, as the war reached its climax. The base was a good place to be, he recalls. The crews got close to each other, enjoyed their periods of leave but every so often such news brought them back to reality. "It is hard to believe that it is seventy years ago now" he recalled recently.

As the planning for the missions continued, the PB4Y-1 plane, as the Americans referred to the B-24 model, was picked for the mission. Unusually for such a mission the plane chosen was relatively new, just five months off the production line in San Diego. The control panel was fitted in Philadelphia, enabling the remote control of the aircraft through primitive television screens. The number on the side of the aircraft was T-11.

A 4th August 1944 US Eighth Air Force memorandum by Major General E.E. Partridge provides a detail account of the overall planning for Operation Aphrodite. It was not released until 1966, maintaining the veil of secrecy and intrigue around the mission for decades after the actual events. "Aphrodite", it states was "...concerned with a system of bombing in which a robot aircraft is loaded with explosives and is directed to a suitable target by remote control from a mother ship flying above." Partridge goes on to write that "...war-weary B-17's and B-24's which have been modified with the necessary control equipment will be used as robots, and will normally carry a load of 20,000 pounds of bulk nitro starch."

The memo was clear that the "success of Aphrodite depends fundamentally on the development of a system of control which is sufficiently flexible and reliable". It explains that the "...transmitters will control the movement of the aircraft, two audio frequencies on one frequency control will control the left-right movement of the robot aircraft, while two audio frequencies on a second radio frequency control the up-down movement of the aircraft". Whilst innovative for its day, today the technology in a children's toy is more advanced than that used in these critical war missions.

Partridge specified that the missions were "primarily intended for the destruction of those targets which are comparatively impregnable". Other factors in the choice of target would include the angle of dissent, local terrain, the presence of a large vulnerable area to bomb, the location of ground defences and the position of the sun at the time of the attack. Aphrodite required almost perfect weather. The mission, it stressed, was for targets, otherwise "difficult to destroy". At 1,000 feet, the operator would put the plane into dive, and the "explosive charge is detonated on impact". Once the target was in direct sight, so the plan went, the drone would be set to 175 mph, descending at 200 feet per minute until it reached an altitude of 300 feet. It would let off smoke to enable the mother ship, which was by then at a greater distance away, to observe its final descent. With that, Partridge concluded that the only obstacle at that point was the weather, writing that "accomplishment of the operation is waiting favourable weather conditions".[19]

Joe Jr left the relative safety of Dunkeswell for the army airbase at Fersfield in East Anglia on 30th July 1944 to begin two weeks of training for the secret mission. He told his parents not to worry, "I am going to do something different for the next three weeks. It is secret and I am not allowed to say what it is, but it isn't dangerous", he said to reassure them, fully aware of the acute risks involved with the mission.[20]

The reality regarding the mission was that Joe Jr well understood that no previous attack had been successful and that until that point every test plane was lost without getting close to its target. There also still seemed to be an unresolved technical issue in the drone too, however, even with that level of risk,

Admiral Horne, would state in January 1946 that the testing of the equipment meant it would go ahead, he retrospectively wrote that;

> "Prior to the flight all material connected with the flight including adequate safety precautions was tested and found to be in excellent operating condition. Although dangerous, all personnel had reason to believe that the mission would be successful."[21]

So the Navy thought it safe enough to proceed. Within days of leaving the south west, Joe Jr was undertaking the most dangerous air mission of his time in England, and one which would put him directly in the path of danger and loss of life.

Training for Aphrodite.
Credit: Military Navy History.

In Joe Jr's last letter to his brother, dated 10th August 1944, he congratulated John on winning his medal whilst serving in the pacific on PT109. He also caught up on family news, discussed his greying hair and shared stories about his fortunes with the opposite sex. He wrote in the letter:

"For the last ten days I have been stuck out in the country, far beyond striking distance of any town. Every day, I think will be my last here, and still we go on. I am really fed up, but the work is quite interesting. The nature of it is secret, and you know how secret things are in the Navy."

Joe Jr added:

"I should be home around the first of September, and should be good for about a month's leave. Perhaps you too will be available at that time, and will be able to fix your brother up with something good. I have already sent notice home about my greying hair. I feel, I must make a pretty quick move, to get something that really wants a tired old aviator."[22]

Joe Jr would never make it home.

CHAPTER 3

From the moment Joe Jr uttered the pre-assigned code words "spade flush" into the cockpit radio, about 18 minutes after the 17.52 hours take-off from Fersfield Aerodrome on 12th August 1944, his destiny and that of his co-pilot was sealed. On Joe Jr's signal, and perhaps last words, he gave remote control access of his aircraft to the formation planes behind, initialising the process of turning the piloted aircraft into an unmanned attack drone. From take-off, the crew only needed to prime the explosive material and wait for the agreed bailout position over the east coast of Kent, where they would be picked up by a following aircraft. The drone, and its accompanying aircraft, would continue by remote control to its 19.00 hours position to dive-bomb its target on the coast of Normandy.

A subsequent report on the mission recounted that there were ten planes in the formation, in addition to the robot aircraft which Joe Jr was in. This included two Mosquitos to monitor weather conditions and to photograph the mission; a B-17 relay plane; a P-38 used for high altitude photography and five P-51s providing close fighter cover. The size of the formation explains why eyewitnesses later stated that their attention was drawn to the air ahead of the explosion. Military aircraft in an area containing numerous landing strips would otherwise have been unremarkable during wartime.

The mission's objective was the Fortress of Mimoyecques, under construction in northern France, as a base for Hitler's prototype V-3 canons. The fortress, close to Calais was code-named "wiese", or "the meadow" and known as Bauvorhaben 711, translated in true Germanic simplicity as Construction Project 711. At full operation the site would have had capacity for twenty five V-3 cannons, pointing directly at London. If completed, Hitler could escalate the terror caused by his air bombing campaign over the capital at whim, targeting huge civilian loss as revenge for the Allied invasion of mainland Europe. Events at that time were moving quickly. Following a series of successful Allied air raids, and the Nazi's gradual capitulation in northern France to the advancement of the Allies, the Germans had ceased work at the site by the end of July 1944, neutralising the immediate threat to London. Experts also suggest that the later use of the V-3 missiles in bombardments against Luxemburg had limited effect, with the weapons failing to cause the widespread destruction Hitler had hoped. The mission was not perhaps as vital as the crew were led to believe. Regardless, the site remained a threat for such deadly weapons to be deployed. Even so, the fear persisted that the V-3 canons could still be as deadly to the home front as the V-1 campaign was being.

Any risk of an escalation in the V-bombings had to be resisted at all costs. Concern ran so high that on 27th July 1944, the British War Cabinet considered evacuating a million Londoners. Prime Minister Winston Churchill MP had told the House of Commons:

> "There is no doubt that the Germans are preparing on the French shore new means of attack on this country, either by pilotless aircraft or possibly rockets, or both on a considerable scale."[23]

The fear of such attacks proved as much a risk as that of the reality of the threat. V-3 certainly failed to materialise in the way feared.

That evening at Fersfield airbase in Suffolk, the two Lockheed Ventura aircraft and a Boeing B-17 navigational plane took off ahead of the Liberator. An F-18 followed, to film the project for the 8th Combat Camera Unit, said to include President Roosevelt's son, Elliott. During the early stages of the flight the aircraft formation drifted from the assigned route from Fersfield through Framlingham to Beccles. It was then due to cross Suffolk, and head directly south, passing over Kent and onto the coast of Normandy. However, after Framlingham the plane was reportedly off course by about 12 miles. Two minutes after the "spade flush" signal was given and ten minutes before the bailout was due, the drone aircraft dramatically exploded above Newdelight Covert close to Blythburgh in Suffolk, with the two crew members still on board. US Navy Lt Commander R. W. Rommel would state that "...the plane was seen by numerous witnesses to explode in mid-air. The explosion was very violent."[24] Joe Jr and his co-pilot Lt Wilford Willy were dead.

Hank Searls, in his definitive book *"Young Joe, the Forgotten Kennedy"* published in 1977, described the explosion as "two high order blasts one second apart". The aircraft following behind had to peel off to avoid the debris, seeing "two bright orange columns of fire and smoke". The radar operator watched as the plane dramatically disappeared from his screen. The plane had exploded instantly killing both men on board and creating a huge fire ball in the sky. Jack Olsen, in his 1970 version of the events *"Desperate Mission"* described the explosion as "...a blinding flash of light, and the bright afternoon sky became incandescent. Where the drone had been there was now a yellow nucleus edged in smoke."[25]

The Eighth Air Force outgoing message dispatched on the evening of the 12th August 1944 bluntly reported that the "…robot exploded in the air at approximately two thousand feet, eight miles southeast of Halesworth". It grimly announced that "…Wilford J Willy CMA Sr Grade Lieutenant and Joseph P Kennedy Sr Grade Lieutenant CMA both USNR CMA were killed."[26] The crew was lost.

The explosion took place above a sparsely populated area of coastal Suffolk fenland, although the size and scale of it provided many eyewitnesses to the events. Searls tells the story of Miss Ada Westgate, who lived in the Shepherd's Cottage in Newdelight Covert and saw "a flash like lightning and then flames in the sky" and heard a "terrific, quick crack". Her cousin was staying with her at the time, ironically to escape the V-1 bombs landing on London during the summer of 1944. The ceilings of the cottage came down and the windows blew out as a result of the explosion. Debris from the plane showered the area, covering a two mile radius.[27] The search of the vicinity began almost immediately, with the area "trodden and re-trodden on the day after the explosion", Olsen wrote, as "American soldiers and officers searched for clues." The reports noted that parts of the plane were "scattered over a large territory."[28] Even today locals still talk about the debris from the aircraft remaining for some considerable time afterwards.

It will never be known how Joe Jr or Lt Willy felt as their heavily-laden aircraft took to the air on take-off. They were acutely aware of the dangers of such a flight, however both men willingly volunteered to put their own lives in jeopardy. Early test flights had not been successful, however even with the high risks involved, they reportedly felt that the mission still had a good chance of success, as later drone flights would prove. Perhaps confident of success or in acknowledging the perceived importance of the mission, they went ahead, risking their lives.

Before the flight, Renehan stated, Joe Jr "…seemed remarkably calm and happy considering the dangerous assignment"; Joe Jr was focused on the mission, and aware of its importance to the war effort, although crew members on the ground had warned him of the risks involved. Perhaps privately acknowledging the dangers ahead, Joe Jr had left a message for his father "that he loved him very much", in case "he didn't come back".[29]

Lt Willy, from Fort Worth in Texas, was not Joe Jr's usual co-pilot and had pulled rank to be on the flight. Willy had helped to develop the Aphrodite project, and wanted to try to oversee its implementation at firsthand. Joe Jr knew that the successful completion of the mission would provide him with the military accomplishment that he craved, no longer having to watch the action from the side-lines. Having waited for the opportunity for the right frontline combat mission to come up, taking risks was just part of Joe Jr's nature.

Just a few weeks after the events of 12th August, in early September, with construction never completed, the Nazis abandoned the Fortress of Mimoyecques, as Normandy fell to the Allies. Kennedy biographer Nigel Hamilton puts the blame on Allied military intelligence who he says "had made a grievous error over the target," Hamilton wrote;

> "Blitzed by Allied conventional bombers all spring, work had finally been suspended on the deep bunker being built there…not only was the site incomplete and already abandoned when Joe Jr volunteered for his fatal mission, but the V-3 gun itself had proved so defective in trails that there were no such weapons to install, even if the site had been completed."

Barely two weeks after Joe Jr's death, the target site was overrun by Canadian troops. The threat from Hitler's V-bombs based on the northern French coast had passed, even before Joe Jr had embarked on his fateful mission. Hamilton calls it a "futile death".[30] History would show the complete failure of the operation.

Writing his report on the mission, on 14th August 1944, in the immediate aftermath of the explosion, Captain John M. Sande, Air Corps, Operations Office, described the events in the air:

> "The Mother ships fell in behind the Robot as it left the field on course, for the first control point. The Mother ships were at 2,200 feet with the Robot slightly head at 2,000 feet. Before reaching the fits control pointe Robot. The turn at the control point was made by the Mother aircraft. Approximately two minutes after completion of this turn at 1820, the Robot plane disintegrated. Both men were still in the ship."

It disclosed that the photographic plane was approximately 300 feet behind Joe Jr's plane and slightly to the right when it exploded. The Mosquito photographer was hit by flying pieces of the Robot plane causing minor injuries with the plane itself suffering "considerable battle damage".[31]

The mystery surrounding the explosion began almost immediately. History now records that the incident caused damage across a radius of a number of miles, and was so large that its impact was unavoidable for many more miles around. However, at the time the local Beccles newspaper made no reference of the incident in their subsequent edition, published on 19th August 1944. Two evacuees, it was reported were found beds for the night on their arrival from London; the Suffolk Regiment saw action in northern France; and the all-important news that Beccles United Football Club had won fifteen of their last thirty four matches was all reported. No reference, however, was made to the biggest event probably to hit the area in a century or more.[32]

Over a year later, on 24th October 1945, the Navy Department issued a press release stating its version of the events. It began dramatically: "both Naval Aviators had volunteered for the dangerous job which led to their deaths." The planes were in mid-air when "demolished" by two explosions, it screamed, "…the cause of which has never been determined". It went on that "many war correspondents knew either part or all of the story but all of them respected the secrecy which until recently cloaked the Army and Navy experiments with drones." The origins of the statement are unclear, especially coming over a year after the tragedy. As was probably the intention, the release soon became the factual account of the events, which would be repeated for decades to come. It was clear to the Navy that the two airmen "…met death heroically in the line of duty" and that the Navy was not to blame.[33]

The first detailed and lengthy press account of the flight followed in *"The New York Times"* in the same month, written by future Pulitzer Prize winning journalist Anthony Leviero. Leviero heavily echoed the words of the Navy release, calling the pair "pioneers"' and "enthusiastic volunteers confident of the success of their mission", but did not link the site of the tragedy to that at Newdelight, nor indeed did the Navy release, and thus setting a pattern which left the locals in the dark about what had occurred there for decades to come. In the report Leviero established for later writers the chain of events that subsequent published accounts tracked. The remote controlled plane was crammed with eleven tons of explosives, he wrote, and the crew was to "check the secret control mechanism, then bail out". After reaching the first of several control points, the plane unexpectedly exploded, with the crew still on board, he wrote. "There were two explosions, one second apart. The escorting pilots saw the drone burst into fragments", reported Leviero. The article gave the first detailed published account regarding the death of Joe Jr, and would provide future writers with an account and timeline of events to base their own versions on.

A further published account of the events followed in the *"Tenth Anniversary Report: Harvard Class* of 1938", which paid tribute to Joe Jr, and echoed the previous accounts:

> "Joe, regarded as an experienced Patrol Plane Commander, and a fellow officer, an expert in radio controlled projects, was to take a 'drone' Liberator bomber loaded with 21,270 pounds of high explosives into the air and stay with it until two 'mother' planes had achieved complete radio control over the 'drone'. They were then to bail out over England, the 'drone,' under the control of the 'mother' planes, was to proceed on the mission which was to culminate in a crash-dive on the target a V-2 rocket launching site in Normandy. The airplane... was in flight with routine checking of the radio controls proceeding satisfactorily, when at 6.20pm on August 12, 1944 two explosions blasted the 'drone' resulting in the death of the two pilots. No final conclusion as to the cause of the explosions has ever been reached."[34]

Clearly, the Kennedy family felt the loss deeply, the start of a succession of tragedies for the siblings which ran until 1968 with the death of his younger brother Bobby, and included the violent deaths of Kathleen and John. Of his brother's death, John would write:

> "It may be felt, perhaps, that Joe should not have pushed his luck so far and should have accepted his leave and come home. But two facts must be borne in mind. First, at the time of his death, he had completed probably more combat missions in heavy bombers than any other pilot of his rank in the Navy and therefore was pre-eminently qualified, and secondly, as he told a friend early in August, he considered the odds at least fifty-fifty, and Joe never asked for any better odds than that."[35]

CHAPTER 4

Back in Massachusetts, the knock at the door came on the Sunday following the tragedy, at the end of a Kennedy family lunch. At first Rose Kennedy was unconcerned at the presence of two Priests on the doorstep of the family's Hyannis Port home, it was not unusual for such visitors. After asking specifically for Joe Sr, it soon became clear to her the purpose of their visit.

The Kennedy Compound (public domain photograph)

The visiting Priests informed the Kennedy parents that their first son was missing in action and presumed lost. Rose, like the rest of the unsuspecting family who had gathered there for their usual Sunday leisure activities was devastated by the news. She later suggested in her autobiography that Joe Sr would never the same again. It has also been suggested that Joe Sr spoke little of the tragedy thereafter, unable to express his grief for the loss of his first born. Indeed he had lost his son in a war he fought so hard to avoid.[36] At the time Joe Sr wrote to a cousin "...you more than anyone else know how much I had tied my whole life up to his from here on. You know what great things I saw in the future for him, and now it's all over." [37] On the 14th August, *"The Boston Globe"* ran the headline "Ex-Envoy Kennedy, crushed by son's death, remains in seclusion", reflecting the start of a pattern as to how the senior Kennedy would handle the deaths of his children. The article continued; "…from the time the family received the Navy telegram the ex-Ambassador has kept to his room. His grief is deep. He hasn't learnt yet details of how the oldest of his nine children – the first son – died."

Nine days later came the official letter from the US Navy. Commander Page Knight, from New York, wrote 'as difficult a letter as I will ever have to write' to Mr and Mrs Kennedy to try and put some context behind Joe Jr's death, and re-affirm to them that his sacrifice benefited the war effort. Joe Jr's commanding officer explained that whilst he "was not at liberty to discuss the nature of Joe's mission" that Joe "…gave his life for a mission vital for the cause for which we are all fighting". Joe, he wrote "… volunteered for a special detail which was exceedingly dangerous' and by stepping forward for the mission he gave his life "above and beyond the call of duty". He paid tribute to the late Joe Jr by writing that:

> "Joe was highly regarded by all of us over here and considered outstanding as an officer and a man in every way in his personal conduct and his high devotion to duty. His clean cut, energetic and intelligent way of life was an example to all of us. Which makes me confident that a nation composed of men like Joe will triumph over any obstacle, He will be missed by his shipmates and his loss will be felt by the Navy and his country."

The letter states that Kathleen had made the arrangements in England for the return of Joe's possessions to America, and that a special mass had been said by the chaplain, in memory of Joe Jr, where the men present re-dedicated their lives to the cause for which he had lost his life. However, other than paying warm tribute to Joe Jr to his grieving parents, the commander offers them nothing in terms of detail of the mission. He concluded by extending his deepest sympathy to the family:

> "You may be very proud of your son for his courage, his devotion to duty, and the magnificent example he has set for the rest of us. We have derived some consolation from the knowledge that he fought courageously for a cause which he knew was right."[38]

The Secretary of the Navy James Forrestal wrote of his regret of having learned of Joe Jr's loss of life. He extended his "sincere sympathy" to the family writing that "the Navy shares in your sense of bereavement".[39] He joined President Roosevelt in sending his regret at the Kennedy family's loss, but Joe Sr "was consumed by hate" at the loss of his son, writes Kennedy biographer, Neil Hamilton, and no number of sympathy notes would alleviate it. [40]

In the days that followed, condolence mail continued to arrive for the family from across the country. A letter on the 16th August called Joe's death "gallant", another on the 18th August to John Kennedy who was in hospital in Chelsea, Massachusetts, following a second back operation thought that "it must be particularly hard for your parents to lose their first born". A letter on 15th August stated that "… it happened while he was on a special volunteer mission, which was an act which one would easily have known that he would be among the first to volunteer for".

Another well-wisher wrote "… in this vale of tears at this time the tragedy is holding the stage – the tragedy of Joe's death. Untimely, tragic, heroic, a hundred adjectives could be picked but your heart and god knows". In the weeks after the explosion, the Kennedy family received dozens of condolence letters, including two from women just known as Alice and Amber. Tributes were also made by the Mayor of Boston, James M Curley where an inscription was made in the city's Fenway war memorial.

Even during this time of grieving, one matter which required attention was that of Joe Jr's will. A $10,000 insurance policy became payable on his death to his next of kin, Mrs Rose Kennedy. All this of course was little consolation for the loss of a son. Lt Willy's widow was paid $15,000 and this too would be paid to her in equally tragic circumstances.[41]

In the years that followed, Joe Jr remained in his family's thoughts. Joe Sr paid Lt Willy's widow a regular bursary and when John Kennedy visited her home city Dallas during the 1960 presidential campaign as the Democratic nominee, she was the first person to welcome him to the city which three years later would forever be associated with JFK and his legacy.[42] Memorials would include the battleship USS Joseph Kennedy Jr, as well as plaques in France, England and a memorial marker at Arlington National Cemetery outside of Washington DC, where the three other Kennedy brothers would eventually rest. A foundation was also set up in his name, building legacy projects in Joe Jr's name in Hyannis Port and at Boston College. A stained glass window was placed in the family church in Hyannis Port. Each year on the anniversary of the tragedy, the family would gather there to remember Joe Jr at a special Mass. John Kennedy only once missed the service during his life, in 1963, when it coincided with the death of his premature son Patrick.

Joe Jr was awarded the Navy Cross, the Distinguished Flying Cross, and the Air Medal. His Navy Cross citation read:

> "For extraordinary heroism and courage in aerial flight as pilot of a United States Liberator bomber on August 12, 1944. Well knowing the extreme dangers involved and totally unconcerned for his own safety, Kennedy unhesitatingly volunteered to conduct an exceptionally hazardous and special operational mission. Intrepid and daring in his tactics and with unwavering confidence in the vital importance of his task, he willingly risked his life in the supreme measure of service and, by his great personal valor and fortitude in carrying out a perilous undertaking, sustained and enhanced the finest traditions of the United States Naval Service."

Perhaps as an expression of his grief, Joe Sr had lobbied hard through his friends in the Senate for such recognition for his son. He went as far as to push for the Medal of Honour, but this was harder to justify as the explosion was an accidental loss rather than one through combat. Joe Sr knew that honouring his boy in this way would help to advance the growing Kennedy legend. It would also make it harder to forget the sacrifice his son had made, and one that he so clearly warned the nation against. In a time of many heroes, the Secretary to the Navy rejected this request as it did not "constitute sufficient heroism". Joe Sr would have to be content with the Navy Cross for his lost son, and it was out of his hands. Perhaps though, Joe Jr's final contribution to the Navy and the family business of politics was when the destroyer named after him joined the US blockade of Cuba in 1962, whist his brother was in the White House. The closest America has come to total war since the end of the second world war in 1945.

Joe Jr's death inevitably changed Joe Sr's plans for his first son to enter politics. Arthur Krock wrote "Joe started planning for Jack to win the White House the day after Joe Jr died."[43] Neil Hamilton argues that John had to commit to a political career as early as Christmas 1944, with Joe Sr already laying the pathway to Congress just months after the loss of Joe Jr.

One remarkable legacy of the death of Joe Jr was John Kennedy's early foray into writing, a journey which would lead to an eventual Pulitzer Prize for him. With the first born child, Joe Jr, lined-up by their father to be politician of the family, John had looked at other ways to develop his career. He seemed to be a natural writer, journalist, or professor and had anticipated such a career until eventually called into the family business of politics. Joe Sr had published John's college thesis *"Why England Slept"*, with some success and such a career path had seemed inevitable for the young graduate. The book would be a personal tribute to Joe Jr and included essays from friends and former colleagues of John's lost brother. Neil Hamilton wrote;

> "Jack's decision to gather together material for a memorial book, honouring his brother Joe as a sibling, a friend, and standard-bearer Taking up pen and paper, Jack now wrote to

Joe's old teachers and professors, his roommates, his valet, his companions at school and college, even his champion, commanding officer, and last mistress soliciting reminiscences he vowed to publish privately as an act of fraternal homage thus to free himself forever from his brother's shadow and his rivalry: As We Remember Joe."[44]

Joe Sr focused his grief on John's emerging political career, whilst John himself "sought to bury his brother with love" through the book, Hamilton added.[45] Two hundred and fifty copies would be privately printed in 1945, but as Hamilton confirmed "no amount of memorials would bring Joe Jr back".[46] Joe Sr himself did not write a contribution for it, and seemed unusually reticent about the project. In the book's foreword John wrote that his "only hesitancy in collecting these essays was that I doubted that Joe, if he had a voice in it, would have approved."

CHAPTER 5

The top secret official investigations into the tragedy took until the late 1960's to declassify. One report was written by Lt H. P. "Rosy" Lyon of the USNR, the most senior officer left at Fersfield in the days immediately after the incident. The base's senior officer, Commander Smith, had been recalled to Plymouth to explain the lost plane. In his report, Lyon summarised the discussions held by a nine man "informal" investigative board, established to "advance the probable or possible causes of the premature detonation of the subject drone". Their discussions included all of the likely reasons for the explosion, however remote that they were felt to be. The board could then draw the appropriate conclusions, or indeed find otherwise.

Thirteen possible causes for the explosion were listed by the board, and each was discussed in detail. Unlikely causes, they felt, included the possibility of flak or a direct hit; friction from the load; radiation; fire; static electricity or the closing of "holding-relay". Each of these was enough of a risk to remain included within the board's final report, but seen as highly unlikely due to the attention the plane received before take-off. Greater consideration was given to four possibilities, namely: the jamming or reception of a stray signal by the cast receiver; the instability of the explosives used; the combustion of gas fumes or finally, simple pilot error. The latter was considered a possibility by the writer Jack Olsen, who claimed that the co-pilot on the flight was inexperienced.

The final conclusion made by the board proved to be inadequate and whilst they pointed the blame towards the possibility of an accidental triggering of the explosives through a technical error, they were unable to say with certainty how that had occurred. Their investigation was important to the subsequent drone flights, which could use similar methods to prime the detonators. Adjustments would clearly need to be made to ensure no further loss of life. The report recommended that "in order to provide further safety factors for the pilots of subsequent drones" procedural changes needed to be made. These in particular altered the way the fuse would be handled; from a remote to mechanical priming and for the device to be set as the crew bailed out rather than remaining on the aircraft once it had been set. No other signals should be sent from the accompanying aircraft whilst the pilots remained inside the drone, it argued. It also recommended the dumping of the aircraft over the north sea, should concern be raised during the flight. However, this report, of Joe Jr's peers at the airbase, remained inconclusive and without evidence. They were unable affix blame with certainty for the explosion.

Brigadier General A.W. Kissner, as Chief of Staff took personal charge of the investigation papers on "the accidental loss of the robot aircraft" and the evaluation of the Aphrodite project, but to no avail in placing blame. Captain John Sande's brief report of 14th August 1944 confirmed that concern was such high that all planes were withdrawn from the operation. After being recalled to Plymouth, Commander Smith, the base commander risked being held ultimately responsible. He set up his own investigation, which even included the possibility of German spies. He again went through all the possible causes, but without settling on one specific cause. They were getting nowhere.

What was missing from the investigation into the loss of the plane, and is still to this day, was the film used by the photographic unit in the accompanying aircraft. Sande stated that the "...photo ship was approximately 300 feet behind and slightly to the right when the robot exploded". The plane was hit by flying pieces of the robot aircraft causing minor injuries. This presumably survived the explosion and would have been reviewed by senior investigating officers. It has never come to light, and would at least show documentary evidence of what took place in those moments above Newdelight.

One suggestion came from an electronics expert based in Clinton, Oklahoma, where the US Navy drone program was located, by the name of Clayton. W. Bailey. His theory centred around the failure of a safety device designed to prevent the inadvertent triggering of the detonation mechanism. Nearby, a new British jamming station had recently opened and could possibly have accidently caused the explosion through its signals. A pin had been inserted to avoid such an accidental detonation by enemy fire or worse an enemy arming signal aiming to explode the drone.[47] Could the priming of the explosive be caused by such a signal, either from the enemy or accidently from the nearby jamming station? Regardless this theory was never conclusively proven, although adjustments were made to future flights so that they were manually primed, and which took place without further incident.

More recently, local aviation experts at the Norfolk and Suffolk Aviation Museum attributed the cause to "a lack of electrical shielding which caused electromagnetic emissions to open up a relay solenoid that should have been closed. When the solenoid opened it set off one of the MK9 detonators, which in turn set off the load of Torpex." Both of these conclusions echo the same cause, a technical error, leading to the explosion. This method of drone bombing was ahead of its time, rushed through during the final year of the war and still unsafe in terms of its technical development and preparation. By volunteering to test such volatile technical advances, it really highlights the risks Joe Jr was prepared to take in the pursuit of heroism.

The October 1945 Navy press release used these investigative reports as the basis for its own conclusions. "One by one, the factors which might have caused the explosion were studied by investigators, but no final conclusion as to the cause was reached" it stated. When checked on landing, the arming switches on the "mother" aircraft had not been touched. Safety features on the drone made accidental detonation impossible. The same list of possible causes was repeated: static, sabotage, flak, a spark or overheating but it states were again all dismissed. It concluded that the equipment and therefore the Navy were not at fault;

> "In checking possible defects, the investigators were brought up against the fact that the drone and its equipment had been constantly checked and were believed to be in safe condition, in all respects."[48]

The Navy's published version of events repeatedly failed to attribute blame, leaving as many questions unanswered as those it resolved. To them it simply became one of those unexplained events of war.

At the time of the tragedy, Joe Sr dispatched his own lawyer to the scene in search of the truth, who went as far as interviewing a local rector to try and ascertain what had happened. Even his conclusions for Joe Sr remained open. He encountered the same problems that kept re-occurring in the investigations; confusion over the exact position of the explosion site, contradictory witnessed statements and a veil of secrecy which would not be lifted for decades, by which time interest had waned. Hank Searls, who has perhaps looked in more detail than any other writer, concluded that:

> "There the matter lay, filed under a red tape top-secret label, proof apparently even against Ambassador Kennedy's connections until it seemed to matter no longer; the mystery described as simply insolvable, a puzzle that Joe Kennedy Sr, would presumably be too busy or weary t investigates, and that no one bothered to solve for him." [49]

As Searls states, Joe Sr seemed to let the question rest at this point, perhaps due to his immense grief. Such a course of action seems unusual for a man of his determination in other aspects of his life. He would never speak publicly of the causes of the tragedy, the loss causing him deep pain. It is possible that through his high powered contacts he was able to discover the exact cause of the explosion, or perhaps he was simply too grief stricken to take the matter further. Could it also be possible that he was afraid of the possibility of "pilot error" emerging as a cause of the incident, with Joe Jr taking his heroism a step too far and endangering the mission? This would tarnish the image Jr Sr had begun to build around Joe Jr, an image useful to the Ambassador in his family's political ambitious and to help erase the lingering legacy of his time in pre-war London. All this is just speculation, the truth will probably never be known. What perhaps mattered most to Joe Sr, and indeed for any parent was that his first son was lost in such tragic circumstances, and no investigation would change that fact.

Could it be though that when Joe Jr's brother John assumed the White House in 1961 that he, by then commander in chief, asked to see the files concerning the incident? Could this have been a way of finally solving the mystery for the family? In September 1962, the President felt immense pride watching the America's Cup sailing competition in Newport Harbour, Rhode Island. He did so from the deck of the USS Joseph P. Kennedy Jr, named after his fallen older brother and dedicated as one of the many tributes to the heroism of Joe Jr. Perhaps then, so close to Joe Jr's legacy, thoughts of the events of August 1944 might have crossed his mind.

CHAPTER 6 – THE SEARCH

The problem with the Blythburgh area is that one patch of Suffolk fenland pretty much looks like another. These large expanses of flat coastal heathland, intermingled with scrub and woodland, make the search for parts of a long lost second world war aircraft literally like looking for a needle in the proverbial haystack. However, seventy years on there are still some clues to follow to find the exact location of the tragedy.

Local residents have a mixed awareness of the incident. Talking to a small sample of them their knowledge seemed limited to a basic awareness of the events that took place, or complete ignorance. Even the local historian in the nearby museum in the beautiful village of Dunwich could not pinpoint the exact location of the crash site, perhaps understandable when there was so much wartime secrecy over the mission.

Previous writers have concentrated on the airbases involved, rather than the site of the explosion. When Hank Searls, who wrote the definitive biography of Joe Jr, visited England in 1977 to interview participants of Operation Aphrodite, he did not say if he went to Newdelight Covert. Jack Olsen in his 1970 account not only included a reference to the explosion occurring over "southern England" but misspelt Blythburgh, perhaps picked up in the Navy statement. Another biographer of the Kennedy brothers' war record, Edward Renehan's account published more recently completely failed to get the location for the explosion correct, calling Newdelight a "town". Joe Jr's brother, Edward Kennedy in his autobiography stated that the crash had occurred over Germany, again seemingly unaware of the exact location of the incident as late as 2009. Whereas Kennedy's mother, Rose, used the Harvard University tribute to Joe Jr in her biography, she again failed to pin-point the geography correctly. She stated though that even they did not know the "circumstances of that mission" for several years.[50]

Confusion over the exact course and cause of the events is long held and started in the immediate wake of the tragedy. The communication notice of missing officers from 12th August 1944 and subsequently the Navy's report of death document, lodged on 15th January 1945, got the location wrong, calling the site of the incident "1 mile east of Blythburgh" and leaving the official record permanently vague.[51] Subsequent reports and articles over many decades unquestioned this information, and repeated it so often that the details became permanently confused and unclear.

However, an eyewitness to the events that day in 1944 was a boy called Mick Muttitt, who more recently wrote his account up on a local community website. Years on, he vividly recalled the explosion, with its epicentre above his Aunt Ada's cottage, the same Ada Westgate interviewed by Searls. The plane blew into many thousands of pieces, so there was never going to be a wing sticking up through the scrubland to search for, however, the aircraft's physical presence very much remains there seventy years on.

Wreckage from the plane was said to have covered a two mile radius. The marker to the north of the debris field is a water tower on a crossroads. The boundary of the crash area then follows the B1125 road south to a junction eerily known locally as the "five fingers", and then takes in the entire area of fenland to the east towards the coast. The explosion itself occurred directly above Newdelight Covert, an area of thicket virtually untouched since that summer evening in 1944. Birdwatchers and dog walkers now keep guard over it; perhaps oblivious to what once took place 1,500 feet above them.

Visiting the vicinity of the debris field, after circling the area twice by car before heading into the aptly named area of Newdelight walks, no obvious sign of the crash site can now be seen. Even the local postman drew a blank when asked for directions. Indeed, apart from identifying the approximate radius of the crash site, there was little else to be seen at first glance. No memorial, signage or obvious physical marker exists. However the area has an atmosphere about it, much like the scene of an old civil war battlefield, you just know there is something about the place. Apart from the site becoming open access land, nothing has changed there since 1944. You can't put your finger on it exactly but the place has the feeling that something significant once happened there, a presence if you like.

Seventy years on Mick vividly recalls the events of that evening. As a young lad he had a ringside seat to the passage of the Second World War, with East Anglia at the forefront of the home allied air campaign. Mick recalls seeing a plane formation of two Lightnings, two Liberator Flying Fortresses and a Mosquito, with several Mustangs following. Suddenly one of the Liberators developed smoke from the rear, and shortly after exploded into a large fire ball, like an "octopus" he says. His lasting memory of the explosion was the burning debris falling to earth and the propellers continuing in rotation on the same axis, continuing to turn but detached from the plane itself.

Mick's account is perhaps vital in attributing the cause of the detonation and finally resolving the 70 year old mystery. The trail of smoke Mick saw was likely part of the detonation process, which was meant to be triggered as the plane approached its target to enable the accompanying aircraft to monitor the drone's final descent. From the appearance of the smoke, it seems that the procedure was accidently triggered and an explosion followed. Whether Joe Jr or his co-pilot was aware of this procedure commencing will never be known.

The explosion took place close to his grandfather's cottage in a small clearing in the woodland. The two cottages still stand there today, creating a little hamlet deep within the thicket. It has the feeling of being lost in time about it. Damage was widespread from the crash, with tiles and ceilings coming down in nearby homes. The shepherd's cottage, lived in by his Aunt Ada, a little distance away suffered similar damage. These hidden cottages provide the only physical marker for the crash site today, without which the area has otherwise returned to nature and as Mick indicated, the scrub has grown up further now than during the 1940s, slowly burying the last relics of the crash underneath it.

Tracking down these cottages was difficult as they are well out of sight. They are located deep in the woods, far from the main road, with the only sign of human life the telegraph poles leading to them, giving their location away. The cottages perhaps do not want to be found. Finding them, mostly by chance after two separate attempts, I start to chat to one of the tenants whose knowledge about the tragedy leads me to directly ask whether he actually happened to be Mick - rather than if he knew of Mick - as one of the last surviving witnesses to the explosion. It was indeed

Mick, who although living a few miles away retains the family cottage in the clearing, with the permission of the local landowner. He greets his unannounced visitors as if old friends, perhaps subconsciously linked by an interest in a long forgotten piece of history. The locals I speak to, who eyewitnessed the explosion, all respond with the same wry smile. Over the years they have been asked to tell their stories many times over.

Mick is like a guardian to the crash site, and generously shares his memories about that fateful evening, bringing the tragedy to life as he speaks. He talks as if it happened yesterday, not as a fleeting moment more than a generation ago. He explains the layout of the crash site, how and where the parts of the plane came down and the damage it did to the vicinity. You don't like to ask about the remains of the pilots, as you quickly realise that the crash site itself is their final resting place.

Mick Muttitt (right) with the author.

I ask Mick about the debris from the plane, and he tells me with that same smile to hold on a moment. Opening his garden shed he brings out a flower pot of scrap metal, burnt rubber and cut wires, which at closer inspection could easily be from a world war two era bomber. He matter-of-factly pours the stored treasure out over a green plastic garden table and the fragments contained within the pot have the feel, weight and sheen of 1940's aviation metal. History is literally spread out in front us, as if a time capsule was just opened. Mick has engine plates from the plane which enables firm identification as the aircraft from the Kennedy flight. Mick talks through the crash site, or rather debris field, and explains that items from the aircraft keep re-emerging even after so many years. Pointing, he says that the plane's exhaust pipe is still visible sticking out of the ground, which again has the manufacture's plate that identifies the aircraft beyond any doubt. Writers such as Searls and Olsen confirm his account as accurate, and well beyond any reasonable doubt.

It is incredible that after so many years the debris from the plane remains virtually as it fell to earth. Had it fallen onto an urban area or land subsequently built on, perhaps by now the plane would be entirely lost forever. The chance that it fell on a rural and isolated location has helped to preserve the fragments of wreckage. However, even today this area of scrubland slowly gives up its secrets piece by piece, and remains hallowed and relatively untouched ground. Two brave men lost their lives that evening, so it must never be forgotten that where the debris fell, so did their remains. This open space acts as their final resting place, in the way that other wartime battlefields do for their dead. Mick perhaps is as much the unofficial guardian to any final remains that fell to the ground there as to the debris field itself.

Mick talks about the interest that has been shown over the years in the events. It was a while later that he linked the crash to the Kennedy family. It took nearly two decades for the declassification of the official files, and the Kennedy's at the time seem to have been given little detail in terms of location. He says that some of the fragments were sent to the family in America and various media interest has been shown. He tells the story of an airman found in Germany of the name Joe Kennedy and the confusion over the appearance caused by this namesake. He also met Joe Jr's co-pilot, who, had it not been for a last minute crew change, might have been on that fateful flight.

For seventy years, since the aftermath of the explosion, there has never been a detailed examination of the debris field. Such air disasters in 1944 were not unusual and the wartime mentality was to move on quickly. The investigators did their job and the case was closed, the only question that remained was what caused the explosion. The evidence gathered would not provide the level of detail needed to answer that question, and the subsequent investigative report speculated on the causes of the explosion rather than the forensic analysis that is undertaken today.

Mick re-tells the dramatic events of August 1944.

I spoke to Mick almost exactly on the sixty ninth anniversary of the tragedy. The search for the debris of the plane in many ways is the final chapter of the mission. Finding it after all those years is like unearthing a locally-held secret, shared only by those in the know and living directly in the local vicinity. The scrubland does not give up its secrets easily, and even with the use of the most accurate map it is difficult to identify the exact area without the help of an eyewitness account. Leaving the site alone is the most appropriate course of action. It is, after all, the final resting place of two heroic airmen who gave their lives for the war effort that preserved our freedom. Advertising the site beyond what is already in the public domain seems disrespectful. Equally though to just forget that it is there perhaps also fails the crew. By not placing a memorial there or one of those well-meaning information boards, as is the way these days, the site remains a secret, open only to those who seek out its whereabouts. People pass every day and perhaps few know the area's significance to American history. It is the dilemma of history.

So what became of the other aircraft which took off as part of the missions? There were ten other planes in the formation on that August evening. Of the Aphrodite drone aircraft, not all were destroyed at targets. At least four of those commissioned were later "withdrawn from use" - meaning they found a natural ending and were not destroyed on a target. One even found its way back to Kingsman Airbase in Arizona, a huge air base which decommissioned aircraft at the end of the second world war. Three B-24 mother plans were used at Fersfield during that period: one was salvaged in November 1944; the second named "Lassie Come Home" crashed at Norwich on return from mission to Hellendorf,

Germany on 14 January, 1945, all but one of the crew lost their lives, and tragically two children on the ground were killed; the fate of the third plane is currently untraceable from the records available. Little physical evidence now remains intact of this intriguing part of military aviation history.

At the age of 90 years or thereabouts, the last remaining veterans from Dunkeswell and Fersfield airfields are still meeting up all these years later, keeping alive for the time being the memories of their time during the war. As Walt Pugslesy put it, their war period in England at the end of the second world war amongst the best times of lives, and without doubt he and his flight colleagues were part of what has become known as the "greatest generation". Walt recalled how the crews "meshed together" and as he put it "they were the best". They probably were. Soon this generation will be gone too, leaving war memorials and history books to tell their stories.

The records show that at the time the Kennedy family themselves seemed unaware of the exact site of the accident, with details emerging only years afterwards. Even articles published after the war in 1945 failed to give out the specifics regarding the location. However, the events which led to Joe Jr's death remained very much in their hearts. Whilst President Kennedy took the opportunity during his 1963 trip to England to visit his sister Kick's grave at Chatsworth house, no such opportunity presented itself to visit the final resting place of his older brother, Joe Jr. As Kennedy flew on Air Force One from his brief stop at Chatsworth on his way to meet with Prime Minister Macmillan in Sussex in June 1963, just months before his own death, he passed as close to the crash site as he ever would, and must have paused for thought at the terrific loss his family had met with during the war years. In his 1945 tribute to Joe Jr, *"As We Remember Joe"*, JFK wrote of his brother;

> "Joe did many things well, as his record illustrates, but I have always felt that Joe achieved his greatest success in life as the oldest brother."

APPENDICES

Appendix 1: Report of the mission of 12 August 1944

Appendix 2: Navy Statement, 24 October 1945

Appendix 3: The area around Newdelight Covert today

Appendix 4: Maps of explosion site - Newdelight

Appendix 5: Map of launch site - Fersfield

Appendix 6: Map of target site – the Fortress of Mimoyecques

APPENDIX 1: REPORT OF MISSION OF 12TH AUGUST 1944

Headquarters

Office of the Operations Office

Station 140

(RAF Winfarthing)

14 August 1944

1. Two PVY-Mothers took off on time – 1755, 1756, circled the field at 2,000 feet. The Navigation ship too off next at 1758, followed by the Robot at 1807.

    The Mother ships fell in line behind the Robot as it left the field on course, for the first control point. The Mother ships were at 2,200 feet with the Robot lightly head at 2,000 feet.

    Before reaching the first control point the Mother ship had control of the Robot. The turn at the control point was made by the Mother aircraft. Approximately two minutes after completion of the turn at 820, the Robot plane disintegrated. Both me were still in the ship.

2. In addition to the above, the following aircraft also participated:

    One Mosquito (516) used to send back weather from the target area.

One Mosquito (569) photo ship covering the Robot.

One B-17 (696) relay ship in mid-channel during the whole operation.

One P-38 (207) to be used or high altitude photo work over the target

Five P-51's providing close fighter cover.

3. The Mosquito photo ship (569) was approximately 300 feet behind and slightly to the right when the Robot exploded. The photographer was hit by flying pieces of the Robot plane causing minor injuries. The plane itself suffered considerable battle damage.

4. Upon receiving confirmation of this report all planes were recalled.

John M Sande
Captain, Air Corps
Operations Officer

Appendix 2: Navy Statement, 24th October 1945

Navy Department

Immediate Release Press and Radio

October 24, 1945

Lieutenant Joseph P. Kennedy Jr, U.S.N.R. and Lieutenant Wilford J. Willy, U.S.N. lost their lives in heroic mission of "drone" plane

Lieutenant Joseph P. Kennedy, Jr., U.S.N.R., son of the former Ambassador to Great Britain, and Lieutenant Wilford J. Willy, U.S.N. lost their lives on August 12, 1944, over England while engaged in a hazardous special mission which was part of the Army-Navy effort to utilize drones (pilotless, radio-controlled aircraft) as an attack weapon against the enemy.

Both Naval Aviators had volunteered for the dangerous job which led to their deaths. Both have been awarded the Navy Cross posthumously.

Their airplane – a PB4Y Liberator – was already in flight and proceeding according to schedule when it was demolished by two mid-air explosions, the cause of which has never been determined despite searching official inquiries.

Many war correspondents knew either or all of the story, but all of them respected the secrecy which until recently cloaked the Army and Nay experiments with drones.

The two officers, whose death was caused by their willingness to fly a plane packed with 21,270 pounds of high explosives, were attached to the Navy's Special Air Unit One, a part of Fleet Air Wing Seven but operating under the United States Strategic Air Forces in Europe, an Army Air Forces command.

Special Air Unit One had the code name of project Anvil, and the mission in which Lieutenants Kennedy and Willy lost their lives was directed against a "special strategically target" —a V-2 rocket launching site in Normandy.

The plan called for the two volunteers to take the explosive drone into the air and to stay with it until both of the "mother" planes on the mission on the mission had achieved complete radio control over the drone, and then to bail out so that the drone, under the control of the "mother" planes, could proceed on the mission which would have culminated in a crash-dive on the target.

Although Project Anvil did not achieve its objective, the effort of the Army and Navy to turn pilotless aircraft into an effective weapon has succeeded. As recently announced, both the Army and Navy succeeded in controlling small target drones. The Navy not only equipped high-powered drones with television so the pilot of the "mother" plane could watch the approach to the target as if he were in the drone himself, but also succeeded in creating a ghost hellcat, a high-powered fighting plane which, by means of radio control, "flies by itself".

Special Air Unit One was organised by Commander Air Force, United States Atlantic Fleet and assigned to work with the Army Air Forces. Three planes were selected for the mission on which Lieutenants Kennedy and Willy died. One was the Liberator drone. The two others were Vega Venturas, twin-engine bombers which served as the control planes and which were brought from the naval air station as Traverse City, Michigan, to the Naval Air Material Center in Philadelphia for the installation of special equipment. The Naval Air Material Center also prepared the Liberator as a drone.

The three planes were ferried to England, where they were based at Winfarthing (Fersfield). Numerous exhaustive tests were immediately undertaken in preparation for the final mission. Sample ladings were made, flight tests were conducted and engines and controls checked repeatedly by specialists. Army and Navy sentries guarded the drone 24 hours a day. A special radio search of the air waves was conducted to make sure that the enemy was not using frequencies on which it was proposed to operate the big drone.

Since it was not possible to take the heavily loaded drone off by remote control, Lieutenant Kennedy and Lieutenant Willy had to make the takeoff and stay with the drone to make sure that both of the two "mother" planes had assumed control. Either "mother" plane could operate the drone, but the presence of two "mother" planes provided an extra guarantee against any possible failure in the control equipment. Then Lieutenant Kennedy, the pilot, and Lieutenant Willy, the co-pilot, were to bail out over England and be recovered on the ground.

Of Lieutenant Kennedy and Lieutenant Willy, the official report covering the incident says: "The Liberator was being flown and checked out by the most competent and skilled officers available. The two pilots volunteered for the mission and were confident and enthusiastic of its success. Lieutenant Kennedy as a Patrol Plane Commander with over a year's operational experience flying PB4Y airplanes as a Patrol Plane Commander. Lieutenant Willy had 16 years total Naval service of which the last three were solely connected with radio controlled projects. Both Lieutenant Kennedy and Lieutenant Willy met death heroically in line of duty."

The flight group — the two control planes and the drone — took off on schedule. Routine checking of the radio controls was proceeding satisfactorily. Then, at 6.20pm, the drone exploded with two blasts about one second apart.

One by one, the factors which might have caused the explosion were studied by investigators, but no final conclusion as to the cause was reached. The arming switches in the control planes, which would have set off the explosives as the drone crashed its target, we both found "safetied" upon landing. Interrogation of the "control pilot" in each ventura showed that the switches had not been touched. Safety features on the firing circuits within the drone made it seem improbable that the detonating circuit could have been set off accidentally from within the Liberator.

Static which might cause an electrical explosion; sabotage; a possible single direct hit by friendly flak; electronic heating of a fuse from an unknown source; gas leakage ignited by an electric spark; and other factors were all considered. But in checking possible defects, the investigators were brought up against the fact that the drone and its equipment had been constantly checked and were believed to be in safe condition in all respects.

Amongst the recommendations in the report of the explosion was "that a second PB4Y drone be readied with utmost despatch for employment against the enemy at the earlier possible moment." The recommendation was adopted, but by the time the second Liberator drone was ready to fly against the Nazis, the breakthrough had occurred and the ground forces had captured the Normandy rocket launching site. So the second drone was flown against the submarine pens in Holgoland.

Lieutenant Ralph D. Spalding of 801 Waddell Avenue, Key West, Florida, was pilot of the second drone. He bailed out successfully through the nosewheel hatch of the drone, only to be killed on January 14, 1945, in a plane crash in the Mediterranean Theatre.

Lieutenant Kennedy was born July 25, 1915, at Nantasket, Massachusetts, a son of Joseph Patrick Kennedy and Mrs Rose Fitzgerald Kennedy of Hyannis Port, Massachusetts. He attended Choate School, Wallingford, Connecticut, before entering Harvard University Cambridge, Massachusetts, from which he graduated cum laude in 1938, receiving a Bachelor of Arts degree. In 1938-39 he served consecutively as a private secretary in the American Embassies at London and Paris. He attended the Law School of Harvard University in 1939-41, and was appointed Aviation Cadet in the U.S. Naval reserve on October 15, 1941.

On October 16, 1941, he reported at the Naval Air Station, Jacksonville, Florida, for flight training. He was designated naval aviator and commissioned Ensign in April 1942, and after eight months duty with a transition training squadron, joined a patrol squadron on January 10, 1943. He was advanced to Lieutenant (junior grade) on May 1, 1943, and on July 18, 1943, was transferred to a bombing squadron. He was promoted to Lieutenant, U.S. Naval reserve, on July 1, 1944.

Lieutenant Kennedy was reported missing on August 12, 1944, and has now been officially declared dead.

He was posthumously awarded the Navy Cross with the following citation:

> "For extraordinary heroism and courage in aerial flight as pilot of a United States Navy Liberator bomber on August 12. 1944. Well knowing the extreme dangers involved and totally unconcerned for his own safety, Lieutenant Kennedy unhesitatingly volunteered to conduct an exceptionally hazardous and special operational mission. Intrepid and daring in his tactics and with unwavering confidence in the vital importance of his task, he willingly risked his life in the supreme measure of service and, by his great personal valour and fortitude in carrying out a perilous undertaking, sustained and enhanced the finest traditions of the United States Navy Service."

In addition to the Navy Cross, Lieutenant Kennedy was entitled to the American Defense Service Medal and the European-African-Middle Eastern Area Campaign medal.

A destroyer, the USS Joseph P Kennedy Jr has been named in honour of the late Lieutenant Kennedy.

Lieutenant Willy was born May 13, 1909, in Newark, New Jersey and his widow now lives at 6424 Garland Street, Fort Worth, Texas, with their three children: Wilford, Nine years old; Kenneth, six years old, and Karen, 16 months old.

Lieutenant Willy came up through the ranks of the Navy to become a commissioned officer. He enlisted in the Navy as an apprentice seaman in June, 1928, and before he became an officer was an aviation pilot. He was commissioned as a Lieutenant (junior grade) on March 21, 1942, and in June of 1942, became a Lieutenant. He also became a leading expert on radio control.

As 500 officers and men stood at attention at Naval Air Station, Clinton, Oklahoma, Mrs Willy received her husband's medal on march 21, 1945. The citation read:

> "For extraordinary heroism and courage in aerial flight as co-pilot of a United States Liberator bomber on August 12, 1944.
>
> "Well knowing the extreme dangers involved and totally unconcerned for his own safety, Lieutenant Willy unhesitatingly volunteered to participate in an exceptionally hazardous and special operational mission.
>
> "Dauntless in the performance of duty and with unwavering confidence in the vital importance of his task, he willingly risked his life in the supreme measurer of service and, by his great personal valour and fortitude in carrying out a perilous undertaking, sustained and enhanced the finest traditions of the United States Naval service."

Appendix 3 – The area around Newdelight Covert today, from the author's collection

Appendix 4: Maps of the explosion site

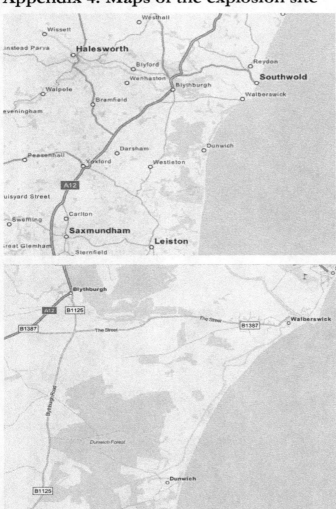

Copyright Open Maps

Appendix 5: Map of Fersfield – the marker shows airfield location

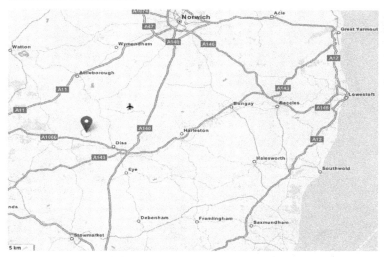

Appendix 5: Map of target site – the marker shows the Fortress of Mimoyecques

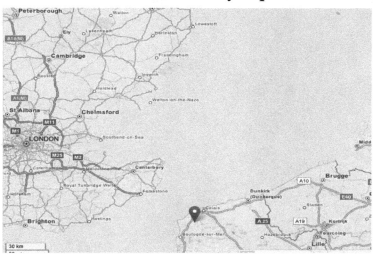

Copyright Open Maps

ACKNOWLEDGEMENTS

The JFK Library in Boston provided assistance and help throughout the development of this project, for which I am grateful. I am also pleased to acknowledge them for the copyright of the images which I have in my own collection, and have used in this publication, including on the front cover.

The origins of this book came from a conversation with Glen Campbell, from the BBC. I was pleased to collaborate with Glen over my previous book *"Kennedy at Birch Gove"*, and whilst filming that project we chatted about the wider Kennedy links to England. I subsequently looked-up Joe Jr's story and knew that as the 70th anniversary approached, it deserved re-telling.

I am grateful to Chris Maines who kindly spent the time with me in Suffolk to retrace the sites involved. It was a day of driving round in circles, as it was hard to find the cottages which provide a location for the explosion as they are well hidden in the wood. Chris suggested that a line of telegraph poles going into the woodland must lead somewhere, and so they did. It was astonishing to then stumble across the cottages and with Mick's help uncover the history hidden there.

Mick Muttitt was a tremendous witness to speak to and incredible guy. He was so generous with his story and I am very grateful to him. Walt Pugsley was also kind enough to speak to me about his experiences 70 years ago, he is one of the "greatest generation" and able to re-create for me the atmosphere of the time at the base. It was strange interviewing him on the phone with a fragment of the very plane he had worked on laying on the desk in front of me. It joined up the circle of history.

My academic mentor for this project was my old college tutor, Dr Wayne Johnson, of York St John University. I have dedicated this book to Wayne, to mark over twenty years of historical collaboration and marble cake.

ABOUT THE AUTHOR

Paul Elgood specialises in writing original short history narratives, re-telling a particular story or event in forensic detail. His well-received first book *"Kennedy at Birch Grove"* was published in 2012 for the 50th anniversary of JFK's visit to Harold Macmillan's country house, Birch Grove in Sussex in 1963. Paul dusted off unseen police and government files relating to the visit, revealing the astonishing and relatively untold story contained within. *"Kennedy at Birch Grove"* featured on a special BBC1 "Inside Out" programme to mark the anniversary of the visit and his later assassination. The material was subsequently used in BBC 2's documentary "JFK: The final visit to England" first broadcast in November 2013. It was also widely covered by the media and has since been commissioned as a West End stage play.

Paul has been active in UK and US elections since the late eighties. He witnessed at first hand Teddy Kennedy's final Senate campaign in Massachusetts in 2006 and Barack Obama's first presidential election win in 2008, standing in Chicago's Grant Park with 180,000 others to see Obama accept the Presidency.

Paul has a degree in American Studies from York St John and lives in Hove, East Sussex. He is on Twitter as @palmeirasquare.

KEY SOURCES & NOTES

Hank Searls, *"The Lost Prince, Young Joe the Forgotten Kennedy"*, published in 1977 is the key source for the happenings discussed here and offers a definitive account of the events and people involved. It was always in my rucksack during the research trips. However, whilst drawing on this important source, I have tried to do three additional things. Firstly, to add to the book in terms of the newly released letters and files which were not available when his work was published. Secondly, the site of the explosion has been of little interest to previous writers on the subject, and has perhaps been overlooked. This can be explained through the lack of precise information as to the location being with-held, and also the incorrect view that most of the plane was destroyed during the explosion. Whilst it was destroyed, the various parts remain on the site to this day, mostly untouched. But you do have to look for them! The story behind JFK's *"As We Remember Joe"* also deserved telling, especially as Joe Jr's legacy was so great on him.

Edward J. Renehan Jr, *"The Kennedys at War"*, published in 2002 provides an overview of the Kennedy's war record. He does not discuss the mission in considerable depth and again does not touch on the site of the explosion. Jack Olsen *"Desperate Mission"* echoes the approach of previous writers, although he helpfully puts the details of the wider operation into context.

Neil Hamilton, *"JFK Reckless Youth"*, published in 1992 created a definitive narrative for JFK's early life. As so much overlaps with Joe Jr, this source has been invaluable for the context of Joe Jr's and Jack's years together as siblings. It also has been drawn on for Joe Sr's support for appeasement, early sympathy for Hitler and anti-war sentiment.

Sources available via the JFK Library have been invaluable. These have included letters, reports and files relating to the period and Joe Jr's war records. These are listed as they were used in the Endnotes. It was a privilege to read the library's copy of John F. Kennedy's personal tribute to his brother, *"As We Remember Joe"* in the place that it belongs.

Operations Aphrodite and Anvil were the Army and Navy names for the secret drone programme. There was considerable overlap in the planning and implementation of the programme so occasionally for convenience the text only refers to Operation Aphrodite. Even the Navy statement on the mission made in October 1945 does the same.

There are a few subtle differences contained within the text concerning timings, the aircraft used and locations. Any inaccuracies are drawn from primary sources or witness accounts, but are still included to reflect their importance to the wider narrative. There are slightly differing accounts of the events described here, and I want to state that I was aware of these minor inaccuracies in the documents and witness accounts, and so they have not been used in error, as I feel they retain wider historical value to this account. These inaccuracies perhaps reflect the secrecy around the mission and the difficulty in obtaining definitive accounts. Indeed, the greatest problem investigating these events was that the initial official reports are incorrect, and traces of these accounts can be seen throughout subsequent work, many of which have failed to question the authenticity of the originating material. All other mistakes are my own.

RECOMMENDED FURTHER READING

Nigel Hamilton, *JFK Reckless Youth*

Caroline Kennedy, *Rose Kennedy's Family Album*

Edward Kennedy, *True Compass*

John F. Kennedy, *As We Remember Joe*

Joseph P Kennedy & Swift (Ed), *Hostage to Fortune, the Letters of Joseph P. Kennedy*

Rose Kennedy, *Times to Remember*

Rose Kennedy, *Rose Kennedy's Family Album*

David Nasaw, *The Patriarch*

David Olsen, *Aphrodite Desperate Mission*

David Pitts, *Jack & Lem*

Richard Reeves (Ed), *The Kennedy Years from the pages of The New York Times*

Edward Renehan, *The Kennedys at War*

Hank Searls, *The Lost Prince*

Will Swift, *The Kennedys Amongst the Gathering Storm*

RECOMMENDED PLACES TO VISIT

Norfolk & Suffolk Aviation Museum
RAF Museum Hendon

John F. Kennedy Presidential Museum,
Boston, Mass
USS Joseph P Kennedy,
Battleship Cove, Mass

ENDNOTES

[1] Edward Kennedy, *True Compass*, 86
[2] Owen, *22 November 1963*, XV
[3] Swift, *The Kennedys Amongst the Gathering Storm*, 214
[4] Thurston Clarke, *JFK's Last 100 Days*, 42
[5] JFK Library, Rose Kennedy Oral History
[6] David Blunkett, *The Sunday Times*, 30 June 2013
[7] Swift, 67
[8] JFK Library, Rose Kennedy Oral History
[9] Edward Renehan, *The Kennedy at War*, 84
[10] David Pitts, *Jack & Lem*, 70
[11] *New York Times*, 17 February 1939
[12] Swift 135
[13] *New York Herald-Tribune*, 16 February 1939
[14] Rose Kennedy letter to Arthur Goldsmith, October 27, 1942
[15] Copy of medical record held at JFK Library
[16] Copy held by JFK Library – Reedy, 22 December 1943
[17] Hank Searls, *The Lost Prince*, 211 – note: parts of chapters two and three are drawn from Searls
[18] JFK Library website
[19] *"Aphrodite"* Eighth Air Force Memo, Partridge, 1944. JFK Library.
[20] Renehan 300
[21] Copy held in JFK Library, Navy Dept Memo, F J Horne, 21 January 1946
[22] Copy held by the JFK Library
[23] Hansard, 22 February 1944
[24] Copy held in JFK libary
[25] Olsen, *Desperate Mission*, 239
[26] Copy held by the JFK Library
[27] Searls 250
[28] Olsen, 351
[29] Reneham 301
[30] Nigel Hamilton, *JFK Reckless Youth*, 661
[31] Copy held by the JFK Library
[32] http://www.foxearth.org.uk/BecclesAreaNewspapers/beccles_newspapers_1944.htm (retrieved 1.11.13)
[33] Copy held in the JFK Library - Navy Release 24

October 1945
[34] *Tenth Anniversary Report: Harvard Class of 1938*
[35] Copy held by the JFK Library
[36] Rose Kennedy, *Times to Remember*, 249
[37] David Nasaw, *The Patriarch*, 12
[38] Copy held by the JFK Library
[39] Copy of letter held by JFK Library
[40] Hamilton, *JFK Reckless Youth*, 668
[41] Copy held by JFK Library – Papers dated 15 August 1844
[42] *Dallas Morning News*, October 5, 2013
[43] Arthur Krock, 60 *Years in the Firing Line*
[44] Hamilton, *JFK Reckless Youth*, 668
[45] Ibid
[46] Ibid, 704
[47] Searls, 264
[48] Copy held in the JFK Library - Navy Release 24 October 1945
[49] Ibid
[50] Rose Kennedy, 256
[51] Copy held by JFK Library – Report of Death – 15 January 1945.

CPSIA information can be obtained
at www.ICGtesting.com
Printed in the USA
BVHW080938010821
612970BV00001B/61